Rising Through the Ranks

Navigating your Next Promotion

ANTHONY FISHER

Anthony Fisher

ISBN-13: 978-0-9978074-3-1

Page composition, content development & interior designed by Rackhouse Publishing

For information about custom editions, special sales, premium and corporate purchases, please contact:

Anthony Fisher
P.O Box 28676
Jacksonville, FL 32226

First Edition

Rising through the Ranks

Printed in the U.S.A

DEDICATION

I would like to dedicate this book to my family.
Thank you for being a beacon of support throughout my
career.

CONTENTS

ACKNOWLEDGEMENTS

To my best friend and loving wife Cherica,
I am eternally grateful for the
everlasting love and kindness you have shown
throughout our marriage. Thank you sweetie for
your dedication, support and endless belief in me. I
appreciate your patience and understanding while we
embarked on this new journey. You have displayed an
incredible amount of perseverance, determination,
and resilience. I love you forever!

Introduction

My name is Anthony Fisher and I like bread! No, I love bread. I share this with you because I want you to understand that everything has a process to rise. There are five important factors to consider for bread to rise, temperature, time, quantity of yeast, quantity of water and salt. The baker must use a thermometer to ensure the sensitive yeast receives the appropriate nurturing to rise. While monitoring the temperature it is vital to keep the time in mind for the yeast to double. If the temperature is not just right the precious bread will take more time to expand. Normally a baker controls the rise by using quality yeast, the quality of the yeast determines quantity of bread produced. The multitasking baker must then add appropriate amounts of water to keep the dough soft and them carefully measure and add the salt. The speed of the rise is often determined by the bread machine but a long slow age makes for delightful bread. I know what you're thinking…what does this have to do with rising through the ranks or navigating your next promotion?

Think of yourself as a baker, your dream job as yeast and the money you receive as the bread. The yeast is the driving force for the baker because it is the reminder that bread is on the way. Without yeast there can be no bread and who wants to live in a breadless world? Within this book I share my personal experiences along with tips for moving out of your current position to your desired rise.

I began the navigation process with mindset because it is the main ingredient for your rise. Mindset is the thermostat for your journey as it sets the tone for growth. Once the mind is set and committed to a positive rise you can began to visualize your success. The successes of my journey has taught me that there is no greater feeling than operating in the success you visualize. Think of your ability to visualize and operate in success as the thermometer. The thermometer monitors the environment and maintains the temperature. As you master your mind it is important to have mentors to improve the likelihood of your success.

The process will require you to face your fears and go the extra mile to develop your gift; If you want to experience new levels of success you must seal every action with a new belief in yourself. Truth is, we all want to rise but the process can be discouraging. The good thing is you don't have to do it alone and I freely share my journey with you. While I cannot guarantee your outcomes I can promise you that if you apply each of the eight chapters you will survive all of the highs and lows along the way.

Imagine that everything you ever wanted is within arm's reach and just 8 feet away. Would you take the steps to grow or remain in the current place of comfort? Would you push past the growing pains and take control of yourself to reach the dream? Most of us would say yes while our actions scream no. The goal here is to rise above all of the doubt and overcome the fear of your success. Once I realized that I could achieve the things I visualized in my mind I carried myself differently. Nothing was impossible because I became the pilot of my life plane. Again, this was no easy task but my success was worth the rise. You are also worth the rise so make the commitment to steer your life in the direction you wish for it to go. Keep in mind that anything worth having is worth working for and your bread is on its way!

Navigate

Use the navigate sections at the end of each chapter to assist in applying the concepts.

Try answering the
Questions to consider ❓ and review the Points to remember ⚠
before moving to the next chapter.

Be sure to record your answers in the Rising through the rank's workbook.

①

MINDSET

I joined the military with big dreams at the young age of 17. My mind was set on becoming an officer, specifically an Apache pilot. In order to become an attack helicopter pilot, one must go through a rigorous selection process. Any soldier may apply for this position, but only those who are best qualified will be selected. The process involves passing the flight physical, scoring well on the Army Alternate Flight Aptitude Selection Test (AFAST) then meeting board selection criteria. The selection board receives thousands of applications from soldiers applying for this prestigious opportunity. The board will only select the "best qualified" and fulfill the vacancies as determined by the U.S. Army. Once selected, the applicant will transition to Fort Rucker, AL. and learn basic aerodynamics of flight school. If selected to attend this highly advanced training; you must complete flight training successfully to graduate with your "wings." Afterall, you will be flying a 30 million dollar helicopter better known as the Apache Longbow AH64D and who wants to miss out on an opportunity like that!

Even though I was young I knew what I wanted, the military was a good fit for me because I was willing to do the work, earn respect and own my career. I knew there would be obstacles to climb, but I was hungry for more in my life. Eventually I made the enormous decision to become an attack pilot and applied as an Officer in the United States Army. This was one of the best decisions of my life and it started with having the proper mindset.

Throughout this book I refer to my experiences in the military and believe that we all make the personal choice to join an army of some kind. Educators join the army of teachers, authors join the army of writers and fathers join the army of parents. While applying the concepts to your life I invite you to think of the army you have chosen to join.

No matter what your mindset, you must conform to these standards to enlist in the military. To enter the United States military, one must:

Be a U.S. citizen or hold a Green Card

Be between 17 years old and 40 years of age

Graduate from high school

Pass the Armed Services Vocational Aptitude Battery (ASVAB) test

Meet health requirements
pass a height and weight compliance chart & complete basic training.

After completing your military screening, passing the Military Entrance Processing Station (MEPs) examination, you finally get the call you have been waiting for. Welcome into the United States military, you have been selected to serve your country. You are overjoyed, and excited and can't wait to get started. Most people begin thinking about their career and possible advancement even before basic training begins. Even though you are starting at entry level (E1) at the bottom making less than $19,660 a year; There are limitless opportunities waiting and the idea alone is almost awe-inspiring.

Now, fast forward ten years and let's look at the mindset of a negative soldier . Promotions have slipped away the thoughts are racing through their mind and the mindset shifts from optimism to negativity. Difficulties arose and somewhere along the way they lost sight of goals and overlooked possibilities. The unhappy soldier begins to feel overwhelmed as the blame game is at an all-time high. *Favoritism pushed you aside. You felt an unfair advantage. You were undermined and got looked over for promotions. You never asked for feedback. You could never move ahead. After all, you had planned to retire and you saw yourself as being promoted (to an E6) earning $53,989 annually. That* *was great but there were still much more to your potential. No one gave you any feedback on what you were doing wrong. You had no mentors to guide you through the ranks of the military. Even though there were countless others who were in authority, they did not help you achieve your next level of success. You never lacked tenacity. You were a diligent soldier with a bright career ahead of you.* At some point the blame game ends and disappointment sets in. No matter what the soldier could not figure out what went wrong. The disappointment quickly turns to anger. The cycle ends with a final

"When you know what you're capable of but lack the right mindset, you rob yourself your success."

blame on Uncle Sam for the lack of promotions, when in fact, the soldier failed to look within.

There is only one thing standing between you and a million dollar rise. This one thing is also the most important hinderance that blocks you from elevating your success to the next level. When you know what you're capable of but lack the right mindset, you rob yourself of your success. This is because your mindset determines your elevation in life. I know it sounds a bit unbelievable but, stick with me for a moment. If you have poor mindset, it can force you and your family to compromise with life. More importantly, it will prevent you from getting the recognition that you truly deserve. Others who are not smarter or more qualified than you will enjoy the promotions and praise while you stand still knowing that you deserve the same level of success.

I'm almost certain we've all met someone whose constantly late for work, calling out sick, or always making excuses for not completing the job. Over time, their negativity causes missed opportunities with job promotions, lateral accelerations and ultimately job dissatisfaction. This type of employee constantly shifts the blame on others rather than being accountable for their actions. Why does this employee constantly seem to experience misfortune in the workplace? The answer is obvious, their mindset has not been trained to always give their best. A change in that employee's mindset could have changed the entire atmosphere and ultimately changed their life. The difference between the choices made by successful and not-so successful people is the key link to a positive mindset. It is well said that a positive mindset attracts wealth and success. Therefore, conditioning of minds is the first step towards success. This may involve compensating negative thoughts with positive stances, as a positive mindset has the potential to accomplish anything. Let's began the journey to your rise by tackling mindset, it is indeed the one thing that's standing in the way of you and a million dollars.

While serving in the military, I knew many soldiers who refused to adjust their attitude. They lacked motivation which caused them to

"When there is no change there can be no promotion."

have a fixed frame of mind. Some of them believed that that they had all the time in the world to achieve their goals. They were given the same opportunities as others but lacked the mindset to wholeheartedly pursue them. They refused to step out of their comfort zones into the unknown which caused them to lose out on opportunities and advancement in rank. Year after year they made excuses as to why they did not get the promotion they "deserved" and now after twenty years of service, find themselves no better financially than before. I am willing to bet that the soldiers I am referring to have not shifted their mindset, if correct their future is identical to their past. When there is no change there can be no promotion. The mind is powerful, especially when we wish to rise personally or professionally. What you think becomes your reality and the mindset you adopt will sustain it.

Mindset is the bridge that connects beliefs and feelings, to thoughts and performance. Everyone is responsible for building their own bridge but, a positive mindset is the universal requirement for growth. Most people who achieve personal goals or professional milestones start with an elevated mind. You have 100% control over this. If you want to increase the value and efficiency of your life and boost to your immune system, change your mindset. A better efficiency can be associated with better performance, health, optimism and productivity of life in general. Shifting your perception is the key to unlock your mindset. It is the secret key that can unlock endless possibilities. You can change it right now! So, let's shift and let's talk about having a bulletproof mindset.

There were two children who were only one year apart in age and grew up with an abusive father. The father had many challenges and obstacles in his life. He believed he would never succeed in business and begin to smoke and drink alcohol almost daily. His mindset was locked in the negative and his situation became worse because of it. Both children watch their father go into a spiral of depression and felt badly for him. The two children graduated from high school and became adults with different mindsets. The youngest child took the path of the father and the eldest child choose to become the opposite of his father. The youngest child thought that there were no opportunities in business because he grew up seeing his father lose hope. He judged his life through the failures of his father and became unable to shift from the path of negative thinking. No matter how many new exciting opportunities came his way he operated in this fixed mindset that kept him stagnant and unproductive. The oldest child operated with a bulletproof mindset for growth and learning. He constantly affirmed the possibilities with positive affirmations "*I am not my circumstances and I will rise above my obstacles*". He shifted the negative realities of his childhood to a positive mindset for growth, for his life to prosper. He challenged himself to create solutions beyond his problems; whereas the youngest child believed there were no solutions to his situation. Both of them were exposed to the same childhood but choose to build their bridges differently. The bulletproof mindset says that nothing outside of you can impact you negatively. When you operate in this mindset you take charge of your thoughts and become solely responsible for your prosperity and rise.

People with a fixed mindset often allow worry and fear of judgement hinder their progress. The fixed mind is dangerous because it is usually rooted in fear, doubt and insecurities. Doubt arises when we allow others to penetrate our mind with their worry or fear. Once the doubt is planted fear begins to grow and the mind is fixed on simply surviving with the bare minimum. Those with a growth mindset focus the most on learning and maintaining positivity. A fixed mind *"When you have* sees effort as a risk, while those with a *a bulletproof mindset, you* growth approach see effort as a way to *bring your game* grow. Both mindsets will have *to new levels."* setbacks or failures but, people with a fixed mindset tend to conclude that they are incapable, and can't change. The growth frame of mind believe that setbacks are a part of personal development. They challenge themselves and find a way around the problem. The amazing thing about mindset is the ability to change it at any time.

The brain is very flexible so you can always change your ability to think and perform. Most times we change our mindset by inserting new thoughts and practicing them daily through actions. In fact, many of the accomplished people of our era were taught to have a growth mindset for endless possibilities. For example, J.K. Rowling faced many obstacles before becoming a best selling author. She was rejected from college as a teenager, lost her mother in her early twenties and married an abusive husband in her late 20's. By 28 years of age she was divorced and diagnosed with severe depression and by 29 she was a divorced single mother on welfare. Even through all of this she found the courage to shift her mindset from fixed to growth and began her writing career. If she would have stopped because of the obstacles she faced she would have never sold 11 million copies of one book on its first day. Her mindset was the tool that helped her rise and navigate through life's changes. The vital thing here is to realize that you can change your mind and picture yourself where you want to be. When you have a bulletproof mindset, you bring your game to new levels.

Let's look at having a proper mindset from a professional perspective. It does not matter if you are an aspiring attack helicopter pilot or nurse, the barrier is always the same. Imagine a man wanting to pursue a career in nursing but knows nothing about the medical field. He knows there would be continuous employment opportunities if he were to become a nurse. He therefore starts the planning process and obtained his letter of acceptance from the university or college of his choice. He is overjoyed, full of enthusiasm and elated about starting nursing school. However, as he began to study the nursing curriculum, he faced many challenges. He did not quit and kept his eye on the end result. He did not blame others for the difficulties he faced while attending nursing school. His mind was set on the goal of becoming a Nurse Practitioner. He continued his journey of success and plowed through the program. Think of the barriers he faced as a male entering a female dominated field. He was able to lock into the growth mindset to seek mentors on his journey to achieve his goals. Eventually, he graduated Cum Laude and began a new career with a bulletproof mindset. What if he would have limited his potential due to the barriers?

Let's take a look at the various degrees in nursing:

Associate Degree in Nursing (ADN) entry level salary $43,680
Bachelors of Science Nursing (BSN) entry level salary $67,790
Master of Science Nursing (MSN) entry level salary $77,536
Doctorate Nurse Practitioner (DNP) entry level salary $98,826

Typical salary for someone with ten years experience can increase by 20%. Nurses can lose out on promotions if they have a fixed mindset. BSN level of nursing is the average level of nursing and Doctorate is the highest level of nursing. Should a nurse stay at the entry level position after 30 years they would accumulate $1,310,400 compared to the average salary of $2,033,700. The difference from the entry level nursing position to the average level nursing position over a 30 year period is $723,300. You can see how the entry level nurse is missing almost one million dollars due to a fixed mindset. Having a fixed mindset stifled the nurse and caused them to miss out on extra income due to lack of education and promotion opportunities. In order to climb the corporate ladder of success, one must change their mindset and always look for opportunities to excel. Shifting mindset can increase net worth and value as a nursing professional.

In the first scenario, the military soldier did not have a proper mindset. He continually blamed others for his lack of assertiveness and did not solicit others for any feedback. He chose to wallow in his misery and disappointments and therefore remained in his condition. Because of this, he did not get the promotion he rightfully deserved. He felt defeated which caused him and his family loose monetary advancements and promotions. In the second scenario, the gentleman who started the nursing program, saw his flaws and continue on the right path. He was able to overcome his obstacles by having the proper mindset and solicited others to help him on his behalf. By having the proper mindset, he was able to grow beyond his expectations and was able to achieve his desired outcome.

A positive mindset is critical to your success! Without it, you might find yourself sidetracked by your everyday routines. You can also become distracted by a meaningless obstacle that can take you completely off course. Distractions push you away from positive progress in the mind . It is your personal responsibility to set your mindset for success. Once your mind is set on the channel of growth and positive progresss in one area you can apply it to other domains in your life as well. If you do this you will reach your goals much faster and find yourself with the capacity to possibly form new and bigger goals.

I remember being on the high school wrestling team, I only weighed 148lbs but could defeat everyone on my team. I did not have doubts about my abilities…"so I thought." However, when I would wrestle an opposing team from a different school, self-doubt would enter my thoughts and I would lose the wrestling match. It happened continuously. I wondered what the problem was and eventually understood that it was my mindset! I knew I was able to defeat my teammate, but fear gripped my heart and mind when it came to my opponents. I had to take responsibility and change my mindset to defeat my opponents. Once I faced my fears and let go of doubt I was able to shift my thought pattern. I became the team captain and was a game changer! My mindset was bulletproof, and it increased my confidence on every level. In order for me to lead others outside of myself I had to learn how to first lead from within myself. Being the captain of my mind was harder than being the captain of the team because I had to consistently out think my self-doubt. This lesson remains true in my life as I continue to rise and navigate daily. You must defeat the enemy of self-doubt and fear in order to rise through the ranks. This is a must as a leader!

Practical steps for mastering mindset

The remedy for mastering mindset includes, gratitude, attitude and belief. You should live your life as if everything were a miracle, and being aware on a continuous basis of how much you've been given. Gratitude shifts your focus from what your life lacks to the abundance that is already present. Studies have shown that life improvements can stem from the practice of gratitude. When you practice being grateful it will make you happier and more resilient. Gratefulness instantly strengthens relationships while improving overall health, reducing stress. The more grateful I became for all the opportunities I encountered in the

"Gratitude sets the temperature for mindset while attitude maintains it."

military, the more opportunities arose. Mindset is directly correlated to gratitude because it allows you to focus on the good for growth. Gratitude sets the temperature for mindset while attitude maintains it.

Having a negative attitude keeps us from being happy and impacts our outcome in life. The key to excellence is attitude - and I don't mean everyone else's attitude, I mean yours. Your attitude determines your altitude: by this I mean how successful you are is determined first and foremost by how you approach life. Without a doubt this is one of the most important keys to success in any and every area of your life. Master your attitude and you will have endless possibilities ahead of you. The reverse is also true - if your attitude masters you, life can be a struggle. A bad attitude can have disastrous results, and a great attitude can have miraculous effects. Rest assured, attitude is the way you show up in life. And how you show up will always impact your outcome in life.

The final component to mastering your mindset is belief, as a man or woman thinketh so is he or she. The challenge is believing that you can renew your mind to believe in yourself. The choice to pursue my dreams was not always easy but the belief I had in my abilities sustained my growth mindset. If I would have doubted myself I would have failed. The level of belief you possess must be bigger than your goal and brighter than your dream. One of the biggest mental traps is self doubt, it is important to always think positive thoughts of yourself. It doesn't matter what others think , say or feel about you, believing in yourself is paramount to your success. As matter of fact, it is quite normal for others not to believe in you because it's your vision and not theirs. Surround yourself with like minded people and always keep away from negativity. Your belief must become an action verb. If you truly believe something, you will act upon it. In other words, if you are believing that great things will come, you must attract those great things by your positivity and belief system. When you wake up in the morning, are you optimistic or pessimistic? If your answer is pessimistic, then your mindset must be reformatted to a different belief system. If you are optimistic when waking up, you are on the right track.

Implementing these tools to change your mindset can cause a shift in performance and propel you to success. You should live your life as if everything were a miracle and being aware on a continuous basis of how much you've been given. Mindset is indeed the first stop on your personal journey to navigating your next promotion. You are in charge of your rise, if your mindset is to grow you will exceed your expectation. If your mindset is fixed you will remain still. Before you move on to the next chapter I invite you to evaluate your mind and make the choice to shift from negative to positive.

Navigate

Take a moment to evaluate your mindset and remember that you are the pilot of your life's plane.

Before moving to the next section review the following:

How can I set and maintain the mindset for success?

What are my current goals, and do I have a fixed or growth mindset?

How do I start each day? Pessimistic or optimistic?

When you know what you're capable of but lack the right mindset, you rob yourself of your success.

When you have a bulletproof mindset, you bring your game to new levels.

Gratitude sets the temperature for mindset while attitude maintains it.

Mindset is indeed the first stop on your personal journey to navigating your next promotion.

Be sure to record your answers in the Rising through the rank's workbook.

②

🕶

VISUALIZE YOUR SUCCESS

Did you know that your brain can not differentiate between perception and reality? Imagine taking a slow stroll in the park one evening. During your stroll you notice a beautiful German Shepard with its owner. The dog appears to be neatly groomed, well behaved and extremely approachable. You are relieved as your mental dialogue concludes that this type of dog is known for having a very good temperament. Eventually the dog is within arm's reach, but your mind immediately shifts to emotions of fear. Memories of a past experience overtake you and false realities cause panic to fill your lungs. The experience of the past was so horrific that you are unable to return to the present moment. Your mind tricks you to believe that you need to run away from the dangerous pet, and you obey. Your perception of dogs is your reality due to a dreadful event. When you are faced with a new dog your skewed perception becomes reality even though it is not the absolute truth. The reality is all German shepherds cannot be categorized as dangerous because of the one bad experience in the past. When you cannot see the reality beyond perception you immediately limit your success. Reality is the present moment while perception is derived from observations.

Now, let's look at the same scenario with the dog and apply a reality-based outcome. Once the dog is within arm's reach you talk to the owner and even decide to pet the friendly animal. You created a new reality to cancel out the limited perception of dogs. Reality can be defined as the state of things as they actually exist. Since your brain can not tell the difference between the two, you can use this to your advantage. There is great power in perception and significant strength in reality. If the two are used properly success can be visualized before its manifestation.

Perception is the ability to see, hear or become aware of something through your natural senses. Your perception can not be 100% trusted because it is very deceptive. Often times our perception is developed from limited observation while reality is created and experienced through participation. Most of the fears or limitations we adopt come from a false reality and skewed perception. If you hold on to limited awareness your ability to visualize and create success will be nonexistent. People with strong perceptions tend to visualize a reality of success years before it

"When you invite success into your life through visualizations you will notice a shift in reality."

manifest. When you invite success into your life through visualizations you will notice a shift in reality. This is because your actions will line up with the things you wish to see instead of the limited things you have experienced in the past. It is very possible to mirror your imagination in real time. Your success is right next to you but, you must visualize it.

One successful person in particular says: create a vision of who you want to be — and then live that picture as if it were already true. In other words, call things into existence as if they were already. Two of the most common ways to positively perceive include vision boards and positive thinking. Both of the techniques create real time visualizations for success. It is important to note that the vision you have for yourself must be outlined for you by you. If you cannot visualize your success you will not be able to maintain it in real time. Do not miss out on success in your life due to a lack of visualization.

I embraced the importance of visualization in my journey to becoming an Apache pilot. I visualized myself flying the prized 30-million-dollar aircraft daily and chills of excitement and anticipation ran through my body. Each time I engaged in the process of visualization my confidence grew and I adopted the belief that it would one day be my reality. I envisioned sitting in the cockpit and making radio calls to the Air Traffic Controller to take off. I imagined shooting the Hellfire missiles and blowing up targets downrange. I even purchased magazines and books to familiarize myself with the specifications before I was ever accepted into the program. I grounded my visualizations with research as I explored the many books on the expectations of becoming a pilot and imagined hovering the aircraft. In my mind, I perceived, I was a pilot before I attended flight school. It was my reality. I never made announcements to the world about the conversations in my head, I simply believed the conversations as I visualized success within. When I was accepted into the flight program at Fort Rucker, AL., it was like déjà vu because I was living my self-fulfilling prophecy. Everything I hoped and dreamt came to fruition. My perception became reality because I visualized it before it happened and prepared myself to achieve it.

Using the tool of visualization can help you achieve your personal goals. If you desire something, you must first visualize it (i.e., promotion, graduating from college, or starting your own business). Do you see yourself being promoted? Do you see yourself being the CEO of your own company? Do you see yourself at the next level? If not, it's time to start visualizing!

"Vision is a driving force for success and momentum and the fire that keeps the candle of hope burning."

When you see someone who appears to have given up on life, the reality is they gave up on their vision. Vision is a driving force for success and momentum and the fire that keeps the candle of hope burning. The door of darkness opens when you lose the ability to visualize your rise. There is a familiar proverb that sums up the theory, *without a vision the people perish* (Proverbs 29:18). Visionless people don't see themselves prospering or going to the next level. Their sight is stagnant, and they become complacent in life. Your vision will be tested but you must continuously fix your mind on the success you imagine. Every hurdle is a hindrance for those who don't see beyond the obstacle. Hurdles can become your biggest asset, but your perception must change. Think of the hurdles as pit stops to your next destination instead of obstacles preventing you from success. If you are unable to visualize your success due to a setback or temporary displacement, frustrations take you off course. You will have to navigate through many pit stops along the path to your rise. Fear will test your commitment to the vision and sometimes the call to rise will test your belief.

While serving as an Apache pilot, I had to perform numerous simulation trainings. Simulation training adequately prepares pilots in case of an actual in-flight emergency. This training is so realistic that it would automatically cause your anatomy to go into the fight or flight response. It's important to have complete control of your perception, (how you see things) or the simulation could be detrimental. We were told to always trust your instruments rather than your proprioceptors if you inadvertently "punch" into the clouds. Accidently, flying in the clouds could cause your senses to go haywire (vertigo). The perception of flying upside down or even backwards could take place thereby causing a major mishap or even your life.

While preparing for overwater flight, pilots had to undergo underwater simulation training experience. The pilots were placed in a mock helicopter above a 50-foot swimming pool. Although I could swim adequately, I had a phobia of being underwater. My fear could have caused me to miss out on opportunities. The pool simulation training was realistic and frightening, but I refused to be controlled by my uncertainties. Fear rested in the corners of my mind, but I silenced it by visualizing my goals and agreed to participate in the underwater training event.

In the scenario, we had a dual engine failure while flying 180 knots, over the ocean. Once the simulated helicopter "crashed" into the water, each pilot understood the actions needed and was responsible for performing them correctly in order to pass the training. As the copter crashes into the water, the pilots felt the rush of cold water enveloping the canopy of the aircraft. The chill of the water engulfed my boots and flight suit. Panic filled the air but I could not stop because too much was at stake. If proper training tactics were not performed correctly, it could cause the pilot to fail the scenario or ultimately lose his life by drowning. I had to take control of my perceptions and senses to visualize my success before it happened. Even though it was just a simulation, my brain did not know the difference between actually flying over the Yellow Sea and being immerge in a pool that was 50 feet deep. As the water rushed into the cockpit, my mind began to race. My mind traveled freely through the pit stops of a doubtful discourse,

"what if you do not egress correctly from my seat belt, or what if you inhaled this water and drowned. What if you get stuck in the seat and cannot exit the aircraft."

The distractors were racing through my mind faster than I could process. The possibility of death was a pending reality, but I had to take control and overlook the negativity. It is normal to have difficulties as we navigate to the

"It is normal to have difficulties as we navigate to the rise, but a shift in perception can change the entire course."

rise, but a shift in perception can change the entire course. I had to trick my perceptions to believe I was calm, cool and collected while under water. With the end goal in mind I began my task to unbuckle the seat belt, remove my helmet and swim out of the cockpit while underwater and in full aviation gear. I am proud to have passed the test and look back in victory even though that was a difficult time in my life. I was successful because I defined my success and grounded it with visualizations.

Success can be defined as the attainment or completion of anything desired. We each have a different definition of success because we have different abilities and desires. In other words, success implies the idea of completing what *you* planned to do in *your* life. Your success may be different from others success and to be successful is to live a fulfilled life. When you achieve certain mapped out goals in life, you can be said to be successful and will permeate to almost every aspect of life. If you attain some level of financial freedom, you can be said to be successful in that area and navigate a prosperous life. There's also a psychological aspect of success related to your mind. You can be said to be successful when you attain soundness of mind. A healthy mind is very vital if you really want to get ahead in life. The key you must remember is to visualize your personal successes.

Mark Zuckerberg, co-founder of Facebook, had a brilliant idea. He wanted to launch a program that was useful to everyone in the world. He started this successful journey while attending college but never thought he would drop out of college to pursue his dreams. Although he was in one of the most prestigious universities (Harvard), this did not stop him from visualizing his future. He launched Facebook with several of his friends and the rest is history.

Sara Blakely, founder of Spanx is an American billionaire business woman. She visualized her idea when she was frustrated from walking door to door selling fax machines. She went home and wrote down her strengths and visualized inventing a product that would sell to millions of women around the world. Initially, no one believed in her ideas, but she believed in herself. She listened to an American philosopher, self-help author, and a motivational speaker, Wayne Dyer who taught her about manifestation, visualization and positive thinking. She was so successful that her company is now a multi-billion-dollar business. Mark and Sara both famously visualized their goals and therefore achieved success.

Here is a big secret! If you never try anything, you will never achieve anything! You have to be able to paint a concrete picture of what success looks like to you. Despite what others may say to you about success, you have to create success in your mind before it can come to fruition. Once you do this, it becomes less abstract and more attainable to you. Remind yourself everyday of what your true goals are, then you will focus on the things you really want to achieve.

Scott Adams, creator of Dilbert comic strip, and author of "How to Fail at Almost Everything and Still Win Big", reportedly visualized his dreams and wrote it down 15 times consecutively each day. Within a matter of months, his goals were attained. Before he became successful he failed at many things, however; he says he learned something from every failed endeavor. "Success is entirely accessible, even if you happen to be a huge screw up 95 percent of the time," says Adams.

Take a look at Jim Carrey. He was an unknown actor struggling to get by in the 1990's. To keep himself motivated, he decided to write a check to himself for $10 million for acting services that he would perform in the future. He dated the check for the year of 1994 and carried it in his wallet for daily inspiration. In the same year of 1994, Carrey learned he would reap exactly $10 million for his role in Dumb and Dumber. Today, Carrey is one of America's top movie stars — and he gives credits to his visualizations with helping him get there. Wow! The power of visualization, he painted a picture of himself receiving ten million dollars, not so dumb after all! He used a visualization method to create his reality. This technique is used all the time to many people around the world, but now it is your time to activate these same tools to get to your next promotion.

What about the media mogul, who pulled herself up from poverty to become one of the wealthiest women in the world, she is one of the biggest celebrity supporters of affirmations. Her commitment started at a young age. She watched her grandmother work extremely hard and she remembers saying to herself repeatedly: My life won't be like this, it will be better. We all know her as Oprah Winfrey and her name is synonymous with winning. Everyone who comes into contact with her, wants her energy. She is a philanthropist and loves to help others. She often visualizes her future and references her successes from having the proper mindset. She is also known for her positive thinking and success stories on The Oprah Winfrey Show — and she even discuss creating her own vision boards to realize her dreams. She has many words of wisdom to her fans but one in particular is — "Create the highest, grandest vision possible for your life, because you become what you believe."

As you navigate your rise through the ranks of life remember to visualize your success. Keep in mind that as you grow your desires may change but the overall vision for your life should not. During the process you will encounter pitstops of fear, discouragement, frustration and doubt. Use the lessons as opportunities to remind you of your vision. Revisit your mindset and visualize success with the goal of rising in mind.

Create a vision board using the outline below.
Divide your board into 4 sections
(Professional, financial, emotional & social)
Jot down your goals for each section using words and pictures. Snap
a picture of your vision board and revisit it often for guided
visualization.

*What do you want your life to look like in the days or even months
ahead?*

Have you ever visualized something, and it came to past?

*How many promotions have you missed out on because you did not
visualize your success?*

*If you hold on to limited awareness your ability to visualize
and create success will be nonexistent.*

*It is normal to have difficulties in life, but perception can
change the entire course.*

*Be sure to review the Questions to consider & Points to ponder
to record your answers in the Rising through the rank's workbook.

3

Integrity
Adherence to moral pri...
...ethics, integrity is re...
...honesty and truth...
...ness, since...

OPERATE IN INTEGRITY

"The choices we make each day dictate the life we lead; to thine own self be true"

Integrity is your ability to act in ways consistent with the values, beliefs, and moral principles you hold. It is derived from integer, the Latin word for whole or complete and refers to a human state of virtue and wholeness. Integrity can be developed over the years and must become so strong that anyone who knows you, knows your integrity. This is because integrity is a collection of virtues, including honesty, courage, honor, respect, responsibility, restraint, and authenticity.

One of the major hinderances to promotion is the lack of integrity. Integrity is the fundamental principle to every promotion. An employer may detect greatness but integrity must be in tact in order to obtain the position. Have you ever wondered why some great leaders find themselves in compromising situations when placed into prominent positions? One could speculate that their integrity was not fully intact and when something unethical arose, it shattered their leadership and caused others to question their character. It takes practice to perfect this thing called integrity. The more you practice, the better you become.

Imagine trying to run a marathon without the proper training. If the appropriate training is not received

"You must build on your integrity and watch it develop into something so special..."

you may collapse after a few miles. even with the right desire and mental attitude. Likewise, integrity does not develop exclusively from desire. It stems from the daily practice of doing the right things. You must build on your integrity and watch it develop into something so special that no storm will be able to shake it during devastating times. The universal goal is a life of impeccable integrity.

Integrity pays no attention to the social class or rank of an individual. The most important characteristic is active awareness and participation in the choice to walk in integrity. You have to remember someone is always watching you and someone looks up to the decisions you are making. Think of the Watergate scandal or the infamous Tailhook military sex scandal in Las Vegas. Both of these instances display how easy it is to lose everything when integrity is not present and people are watching. .

In the Watergate scandal, President Richard Nixon used his leadership to cover one of the largest "cover ups" in the United States history. All throughout the White House, wiretaps were secretly placed to hear secret conversations. These conversations could change history if revealed. June 17, 1972, the police arrested five burglars at the office of the Democratic National Convention (DNC) inside the Watergate complex. Nobody ever imagined that the four burglars were formerly working for the Central Intelligence Agency (CIA) against the powerful Fidel Castro in Cuba. After hours of surveillance and investigating, America's deepest cover-up revealed the President of the United States had direct involvement in the Watergate scandal. The president actually financed the wiretapping and the White House break-in through illegal laundered campaign contributions. The shocking news of our great leader being involved in illegal activities changed the course of how we do business in politics. It made Americans suspicious of the government and if this took place what else has the government being hiding from the people. This scandal led to the discovery of numerous abuses of power by members of the Nixon administration. After careful investigation, an impeachment process began against the president of the United States of America. The results of the investigation indicted 69 people and 48 of those were found guilty in which many of whom were top Nixon officials. We all know the rest is history and President Nixon resigned. The morale of the story, one could be in a position of power but if he or she lacks integrity everything will eventually come crumbling down!

Despite societal forces that test integrity, most people agree that we deserve a world that values truth, honesty, and justice. As the basis of social harmony and action, integrity plays a critical role in civil society as well as democracy. When you are left alone on the job, will you do the right thing in the absence of leadership? If the answer is yes, you are well on our way to rising through the ranks.

Do you remember the Tailhook fiasco that took place in 1991? The Tailhook Association is a private organization that sponsors the Tailhook Symposium which is a reunion of former marine and navy aviators. Well, in 1992, a female Navy Lieutenant claimed while she was attending this symposium, she was groped and forced to pass through many of the officers. She revealed this was not the first incident and it happened on numerous occasions. After a seven month investigation, by the Naval Criminal Investigative Service, more than 140 cases were uncovered and misconduct against 80-90 women. The Tailhook association repeatedly tried to defend their case and discredit the female for such allegations to no avail. The female victim actually sued the association and it settled out of court. As a result of this fiasco, the Secretary of the Navy ordered disciplinary action against 70 individuals. Here was the shocker...some of the individuals who were exposed were high ranking officers in the Navy. As the Tailhook story began to spread, senior officers retired or had their careers ruined. After the final investigation 14 admirals and nearly 300 naval aviators were damaged by the sex scandal.

General Petraueus was an awesome Army General who was able to rise through the ranks quickly. He was well known at Fort Campbell, KY and the 101st Airborne Division during the 90's. While stationed at Fort Campbell, he was shot during a training exercise and did not allow that to stop him from progressing in the ranks. He eventually became the Commander of the Multi-National Force in Iraq in 2008 and led a successful campaign. He retired and became the CIA director. Unfortunately, his integrity was placed in jeopardy when faced with a sex scandal with one of his interns. This ultimately led to his resignation which caused him to lose the respect of his wife, global leaders and many others who followed in his footsteps. You have much at stake if you lack integrity. No matter your rank in the military or advancement in the corporate ladder of success, if you continue to have integrity issues you are placing your career and family in jeopardy. A lack of integrity will ultimately ruin your good name, reputation and chances of greater success. In order to rise through the ranks, you must learn how to become a person of integrity. Your integrity must be bulletproof!

"A lack of integrity will ultimately ruin your good name, reputation and chances of greater success.."

Imagine leaving a plate of freshly baked chocolate chip cookies on the table in front of a child who loves cookies. The child is aware that the cookies are for after dinner but the temptation to partake builds as the aroma fills the room. No one is watching the young child and thoughts of enjoying one or two of the cookies seem to fill their little mind. Do you think this child will be tempted to eat one of the cookies without asking? While we may never know the end result the fact remains that there are only two option. The child can eat a cookie without permission or act in integrity and wait until the appropriate time and permission is granted. The cookie challenge may not be difficult for you because you must pass your specific test in order to develop individual integrity.

As a teenager, I just assumed that I would wake up one day and I would be a man of integrity. Over the years, my parents taught me how to be a man of integrity. Integrity, however, is not a value that is simply passed on. It's something that must grow inside us. This is the furthest from the truth. Your integrity must be strengthened by trials and test so you are ready when placed in a leadership position. The process of developing and instilling integrity begins by understanding three important steps: drawing the line, avoiding evil and being accountable.

——————— Draw the Line ———————

As a young recruiter, I had to make a decision whether to allow a young man to enlist in the military or follow his dreams of going to college. This young man was very enthusiastic about the military and eager to join. He passed the ASVAB (the military test that qualifies applicants to join) and scored rather high. However, he also had a full academic scholarship to Georgia State University. I had to choose to do the right thing. I could have easily allowed him to enlist in the military and received the recognition and accolades of being a stellar recruiter. However, I choose to use my influence to help him make a wise decision. He needed to know the other options that were readily available for him. Needless to say, he went to college and is living the life he desired. Integrity is not being selfish, but doing the right thing not only for yourself but for others as well. When you draw the line you set the bar for what you will allow. Clear boundaries are useful to avoid blurred lines and character accusations. The first step in drawing the line is to visit your ethics. Define

"The first step in drawing the line is to visit your ethics. Define what is ethical for you and make a personal agreement to only partake of the identified behaviors."

what is ethical for you and make a personal agreement to only partake of the identified behaviors. Once your ethical standards are set be sure to courageously draw the line when test arrive. Honesty is one of the most important characteristics of integrity for me. The young man may have been a great recruit but my ethical duty was to ensure he knew the truth in all of his options. What if I would not have been truthful with him? One single act could have ended his life and robbed others of the impact they were to receive from him. Integrity in all situations benefits not only you but others who are assigned to receive from you. Any position you may ever pursue or land depends on your ability to clearly draw the line. You have the pencil and can erase and restart as you need to but take the first step to bullet proof integrity and create your line!

⊘ Avoid Evil ⊘

"Hear no Evil, Speak no evil, See no evil"

Evil communication corrupts good manners. Watch for people who use smooth speech and flattering words to deceive others. Avoid partnerships with those who believe that "*it's okay as long as you don't get caught,*" or "*it's not that bad, every one's doing it.*" If your goal is to rise to a rank of leadership then it is important to teach others how to lead by

Apply the following two important questions when defining evil include: does it manipulate others or is it intentionally deceiving anyone?

example. Evil people mislead others and influence bad habits because they are great at deception manipulation. Doing wrong is never right and bulletproof integrity understands the responsibility to practice right living on every level.

Apply the following two important questions when defining evil include: does it manipulate others or is it intentionally deceiving anyone? Remember the previous examples of the Watergate scandal; What if the former president would have asked the two questions prior to engaging in the behaviors? History would have played out differently and accusations of evil would have been avoided. While there is no one size fits all solution for evil the process for overcoming it is simple. When faced with temptations use your intuition and chose what is right to avoid evil. Again, there will always be test after a lesson so make the commitment to choose to do what is right- always!

Be Accountable

Let's make a deal.. Starting now you alone are responsible for your actions...no more shifting the blame on others. In order to develop as a leader, you must take responsibility for what goes right and what goes wrong. Don't be the leader who often attempts to appear perfect and never make mistakes. Never lie to yourself so that you can always remain credible. Subordinates are looking to your leadership and are often assessing how you react even when they know you are wrong in a situation. If you make a mistake, own up to your mistake. Hold yourself accountable with the understanding that how you handle the situation (even if you "messed up"), can strengthen how others view you as a leader. On the other hand, if you make a mistake and desperately try to cover it up you will end up looking foolish. It is much easier to admit fault and fix the wrong than to recover from losing credibility with your peers and colleagues. Lack of accountability can ultimately tarnish your name and you must take responsibility for the choices you make. No great leader shifts blame on others and then expect others to view them as their fearless leader.

As a pilot in command, I was accountable for a $30 million dollar aircraft and everything that happened inside the cockpit. Regardless of who made the mistakes or what errors were made, I was accountable for any mishap that occurred. This is critical in developing any new leader in a leadership role. You will be tested as a leader. When you know you are responsible for the outcomes, you are more aware of the factors that can contribute to a mishap. If you do not pass the small hurdles as a leader, you will not be prepared to lead by example. Use the "do unto others" mantra as it relates to integrity to remain on track. Before saying or doing anything take a moment to ask yourself " am I doing unto others what I would want done to me" ? If your evaluation results in a strong yes then continue on with the behavior. If your evaluation reveals a flaw in your integrity take time to fix the problem and grow as the leader of your life. Accountability is indeed a key factor when rising through the ranks, navigate with integrity!

Here is a secret that can literally change your life. Your integrity does not have to take a back seat for you to rise. This has been played out more publicly in the U.S. politics, military and other high powered careers. People do not have to experience dishonesty, or bullying for your needs to be fulfilled. Remember that integrity is a silent guide that lifts you to the position and allows you to retain it.

The consequences of ignoring integrity are real, and the psychological damage can run deep, even for those who sit silently on the sidelines. Like second-hand smoke, the effects of disrespect and dishonesty often seep invisibly into the bodies and minds of those around. As Gandhi so eloquently said, "To believe in something, and not to live it, is dishonest." Always activate integrity by being true to yourself! You must be true to yourself in order to be an effective leader. Sometimes it may seem a lot easier to just go with the flow, but great leaders learn how to lead and influence others like water flowing over a rock. Water can move and overcome any obstacle which stands in its path. While rocks have a tendency to stand still until moved by something or someone. If you view people as a rock and you are the water, this correlation will help you determine how to adjust your style of leadership. Are you the water or the rock in leadership?

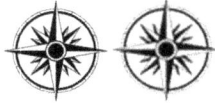

Activity

Reflect on a time when your integrity was on the line or in question. Think about what caused you to be in this predicament and answer the questions below:

Were you caught doing something wrong?
If so, what were the consequences?
If you were not caught, how long did you continue to compromise your integrity?
What should you do differently in the future?

What do I value and believe?

Am I acting in integrity daily?

Am I the water or the rock in leadership?

Integrity is your ability to act in ways consistent with the values, beliefs, and moral principles you hold.

The consequences of ignoring integrity are real, and the psychological damage can run deep.

*Be sure to review the Questions to consider & Points to ponder to record your answers in the Rising through the rank's workbook.

SEEK MENTORSHIP

All of the greatest players within any sport have coaches/mentors. Mentorship is the common denominator between successful men like Lebron James, Michael Jordan, Kobi Bryant. Each of them have identified someone to drive them to achieving their best. There are three valuable mentors in my life that "pushed" me to success. My father Mr. Nathaniel Fisher is a loving man that instilled greatness in me. He has a strong faith in God, and always told me that I could accomplish anything if I believed in myself. The second mentor is Mr. Ben Coarde, he is a man of generosity and courage. Mr. Coarde and I developed such a meaningful relationship and he gave so much of himself which led others to want to emulate him. I was captivated by his military service and knew one day I would join the military. My goal became a reality because of his mentorship. When he shares some of his experiences while serving in the Air Force I listened intently. The wisdom and insight he shared assisted in my rise as a successful Army Aviation Officer. The last mentor I mention commanded thousands of airmen, soldiers, sailors and marines while stationed at Scott Air Force Base, IL. Lieutenant General Kenneth R. Wykle had a positive impact in my life while working under his leadership and observing his daily routines. One of the biggest take aways form his mentorship was the consistent demonstration of leadership at a higher level. Although he had great military rank, he showed such dignity and grace for all mankind. No one felt unimportant in his presence and I learned the meaning of how to treat others regardless of their socioeconomic background, rank, status, or position one hold's in life. While admiring him, I wanted to exude the same professionalism and confidence he displayed. My mentors were a key element to my successful journey.

Mentors are an important part of growth. In order to overcome obstacles in one's life and become fruitful, it is necessary to have mentors and coaches. Most successful businessmen and women or high ranking officers have had someone in their life to help them reach their full potential. You are no different; If you want to climb the ladder of success, one of the fastest ways to achieve this goal is to find a mentor. Steering through the ranks requires heeding the advice of others to avoid unnecessary pitfalls. Find someone who has already achieved the level of success you are pursuing. You may want to consider the professional advice of others if you are unsure how to tackle an assignment or want to talk through an interesting job

"Someone has already endured the trials and tribulations for you and would like to guide you through them."

offer. Having a few mentors to help you along the way is paramount to your success. Good mentors are similar to life coaches because they guide you along the way. Good mentors do not pamper you or tell you what you want to hear. This is because they want to see you grow and achieve the success you have identified.

If you choose not to have a mentor, you run the risk of taking the hard road. Someone has already endured the trials and tribulations for you and would like to guide you through them. Why re-invent the wheel, when it's already made? There is literally no need to stress, or over complicate the matter at hand. Think of a mentor as an investment in your life. When financial investments are made, everyone looks for the return on investment (ROI), the same is true with finding a proper mentor. The ROI is huge when you have connected with the right one. Not having a mentor can cause you to lose a great deal of money!

A trusted mentor can help you gain valuable advice, develop your knowledge and skills and improve your communication. Mentors offer valuable insight into what it takes to get ahead. They can be your guide and "sounding board" for ideas, helping you decide on the best course of action in difficult situations. You may learn shortcuts that help you work more effectively to avoid "reinventing the wheel." They can help you identify the skills and expertise you need to succeed. They may teach you what you need to know, or advise you on where to go for the information you need. Just like your mentor, you may also learn to communicate more effectively, which can further help you at work.

The process for finding a mentor is a little different for everyone; some mentoring relationships happen naturally, while others require extra effort. It's not always easy to find mentors. Who should you turn to? More importantly, how do you approach them and build relationships with them over time? Let's look at the three type of mentors you may encounter at different phases of life.

The "1 Year guide" Mentor

Think about your short-term career goals: Where do you want to be at this time next year? Look for a person who's currently there, and seek him out to be your "where I want to be in a year" mentor. Ideally, this person is someone who's been in your shoes and can easily relate to your current experiences. This type of mentor is great when you need advice on the little things, like the best way to approach a project. Especially if he or she works within your company, and can give you the insider scoop. Keep in mind that the most important conversations should include wisdom on the specific tasks you should take to get to the next level.

If you work for a large organization, you can usually find this kind of mentor just by socializing and getting to know people in your office. If you work for a smaller company or department, it can be a bit harder but don't be afraid to reach out to people in your network or at local job fairs. The opportunity is tremendous and networking is a key to your success. Once you find a potiential, start the relationship by taking the soon to be mentor out to coffee and asking about their current role and responsibilities. Get the details on how they obtained their current position in the company. Be sure to take in any advice they offer during the disclosure and ask questions. After that, keep it casual and hopefully you'll be comfortable enough to reach out to them again as deep questions or issues arise. Keep in mind that the year one mentor may not be a life long guide and your vision may outgrow

"Keep in mind that the year one mentor may not be a life long guide and your vision may outgrow them."

them. If this occurs its important to keep a good working relationship with them.

The Five-Year Mentor

While a one-year mentor is great for the day-to-day stuff, it's also good to have a "where I want to be in five years" mentor. With a bit more experience under their belt, this person can offer you advice on advancing within your company or field, including the short-term goals you should be setting in order to get there. When you're seeking out this person, look at mid- to senior-level managers who are well-known and respected within your company. Keep in mind that you may meet your five year mentor during your one year journey. If you have an idea of someone who's in your dream role, but don't know them personally, find a colleague who does. Stepping outside of your comfort zone is a big part of navigating to your next promotion so don't be afraid to ask for an introduction. You must make your vision happen in real time and shift your mindset from being a bother to maximizing every opportunity. One of the biggest pitfalls of the mentoring relationship is mentees yield to feelings of "being a bother". If your mentor is committed to your success they will carve out time to connect and the process will flow organically.

It is important to your relationship with the five year mentor a bit more buttoned-up. Once you make your move and ask for a meeting treat it almost like an informational interview. Have some questions ready to ask about their career path and how they moved within the ranks of the company. Then, see if they would be willing to meet with you every quarter or so to discuss your career path. Most importantly, keep things professional, and make sure you don't bring office drama into the mix. Keep your destination in mind while being present on the journey.

The Career Mentor

The final type of mentor should be a "what do I want to do with my career" advisor. This person may not be in your company, but should work (or have worked) in your industry. The mentor should be someone who knows the tools of the trade and can consult you on big events and decisions, like switching jobs, working abroad, or exploring other career opportunities.

This type of mentor may take longer to find and will likely change throughout your career. This relationship will also probably grow organically when you're first starting out, it may be your favorite professor from college, or, later down the road, it may be a former colleague or boss. You can definitely have more than one of these types of mentors because it never hurts to have a few great minds on your team. While it's good to check in with this mentor regularly, it's most important to consult with them during times of transition. Share your goals, and ask for help in figuring out how to get there, seek their advice on any major steps you're considering, like going to grad school or accepting a new position.

Throughout your career, you may experience many people turning to you for help and advice. But, by being strategic and identifying a few key mentors to be your "board of advisors," you'll make sure that advice is always steering you in the right direction.

Again, you can learn new ways of thinking from your mentor, just as your mentor can learn from you. Your mentor can offer an opportunity to expand your existing network of personal and professional contacts. A mentor helps you stay focused and on track in your career through advice, skills development, networking, and more.

Tigers Woods was one of the best golfers in the world at the age of 21. The fame and fortune followed him after each tournament. He won a total of 14 major championships. He had a great mentor in his life who constantly told him he was great and could overcome any obstacle with practice and hard work. His mentor happened to be his father. His father, Earl, had such an influence in his life. A retired Army special forces Officer, he had a no nonsense approach to teaching and mentoring. He would push Tiger to his limits making him master his trade. Tiger knew his father would not steer him wrong and he took his father's advice to heart. Something drastically changed in Tiger's life. What happened with Tiger Woods? Well, his mentor (father) passed away and it seemed like everything went through a downward spiral. After losing his mentor, Tiger started drinking heavily, received several DUIs and started abusing women. He was caught in several scandals while married. Now, one of the greatest household names in America has been tarnished. He would be known as an adulterer and woman abuser. He was featured on TMZ (thirty-mile zone), which is an American syndicated entertainment and gossip news television show, as a man that had no family values.

What was the cause of his demise? He lost his mentor. His father, Earl Woods preceded him in death which was life changing for the master champion world top golfer. Losing his mentor

"without good direction people loose their way."

was not only devastating, but costly. After the lost of his father, Tiger financial portfolios plummeted. He had to pay fines and court fees for the numerous scandals and affairs which ultimately costed him his marriage and his good reputation with his fans.

A good mentor is equavelent to a tour guide or realtor. They assist in exploring the possibilities with knowledge of the history. One of my favorite proverbs quotes it nicely in saying, *"without good direction people loose their way"*. This is true in every of life, everything is better with directions and mentors. Mentoring is not a easy solution to rising and it will require you to be patient with the process. Don't jump to conclusions if things don't turn out the way you hope initially and keep an open mind. Most of the best opportunities in life happen when we take the limts off of our mind. If you want to attract a good mentor keep your mind free and clear of assumptions and negativity. Most of all, try to keep your goal in mind at every phase of the partnership.

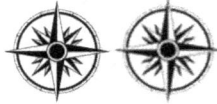

Think about the mentors in your life and answer the questions below.

Who is my 1 year mentor?
Who is my 5 year mentor?
Who is my career mentor?

Steering through the ranks requires heeding the advice of others to avoid pitfalls

You can learn new ways of thinking from your mentor, just as your mentor can learn from you

Without direction people loose their way.

*Be sure to review the Questions to consider & Points to ponder to record your answers in the Rising through the rank's workbook

⑤

FACE YOUR FEARS

So you've analyzed your desires and determined the life you want to have. You revisit your mindset often and even posture yourself in the seat of positivity but, can't seem to move ahead. I am willing to bet that the problem is fear. Fear will prevent you from reaching your destination and must be overcome if you want to succeed in anything. Fear injects psychological toxins into our subconscious that hold us still. When we do not face our fear it becomes like handcuffs that restrain our ability to achieve a goal. Fear is a master manipulator and even when you know it isn't real it can be hard to move beyond it. This perceived fear plays games with our minds, robbing us of any rational thoughts we need to cherish in order to move ahead. If you want to unlock your potential to rise through the ranks you must face your fears.

I had to personally deal with my own fears while attending aviation school. In flight school, we are told that we will take our solo flight after logging only 15 hours of flight time. This seem like an unusually small amount of flight time before being released to fly on our own. Nevertheless, we were going to fly whether we wanted to or not so we had to face our fears!

There are times that you think you are almost touching happiness and holding it tightly, but you can't be sure how to overcome fear. When this kind of fear is strong, some sort of negative feeling is coming your way that doesn't allow you to let go things which would be able to accelerate your path to success. You believe you are unworthy of any positive outcomes or recognition you will receive as a result of your achievements, so why even try? You feel afraid of failing or making mistakes that you refuse to even make the first attempt. Because your self-confidence is undermined, you begin to doubt your own abilities to execute a task. There is very little effort made to attempt a project. This cycle of fear will continue unless you take the steps to overcome it.

The fear of flying without an instructor made me very uncomfortable because it was outside of my comfort zone. I was use to all decisions being made with the input of my stick buddy while we attempted to fly this aircraft. I had to prepare myself both mentally and physically in order to pull it off. My mindset was shaky but I visualized my success and did my best to activate my self confidence. I gave myself pep talks as mental preparation before each flight and soon gained the confidence of flying. Eventually it became as easy as riding a bike.

When the day arrived the instructor gave us a word of encouragement as he departed the helicopter. He provided comfort by reminded us that he would be in the Air Traffic Control tower if we needed him. Even with confidence I thought to myself, *"Are you seriously going to leave us in this helicopter with only 15 hours of training"*? My fear took over and as the final seconds passed I became nervous because I did not feel ready. With my anxiety on overdrive I took a moment to take in the reality and unlock the truth that I could indeed do this. I was one of two newly assigned student pilots attempting to successfully fly a traffic pattern at 1,000 feet, and land the helicopter without the instructor pilot. I look back in retrospect and realize that nothing good comes from comfort zones. In order to grow, one must become uncomfortably brave even if it makes you sweat! We conquered the flight and I overcame my fear, it wasn't as real as my emotions made it seem.

When fear is perceived, the portion of the brain involved in fear automatically reacts. It triggers behaviors such as a racing heart, anxiety, or sweaty palms. If the fear is related to doubts about your own ability, the fear will allow you to come up with an excuse why you can not accomplish

"Anxiety can stifle who you are and cause you to second guess your future."

your task. The process of fear is entirely subconscious. You are driven to think, believe, and act based upon the fear you initially perceived. If the perceived fear is funneled through unfavorable past experiences, the subconscious mind injects even more doubt and eventually you feel unable to make it past the first step. Anxiety can stifle who you are and cause you to second guess your future. Overcoming this phenomena called fear is paramount to your success especially as it relates to your next promotion!

Most people will do anything within their power to avoid pain or discomfort in life. Doing this only enables you to give in to the fears we are fed by the subconscious. This fear prevents you from even attempting the first move. There may be times that your ambition motivates you past the first step; but the discomforts and doubts keep you still. Fear can be so much more powerful than your own ambitions and keep you from fully following through. In order to rise through the ranks, you must have self-confidence. This confidence can come by positive affirmations, removal of negative thoughts and believing in yourself.

Over time fear eats away at your self-confidence and if unchecked it can erode who you are and what you believe. You begin to come up with excuses why things can't get done and play the victim role. When you submit to fear you may feel sorry for yourself and even become depressed. Great ideas are sabotaged and possible promotions are ignored and eventually you become totally bound by fear. If I would have submitted to my fear on the independent flight the outcome may have been different. I held myself to a higher standard and eliminated the fear before it became bigger than my self esteem. The affirmations I used were effective in overcoming the fearful thoughts and operating in success. Your confidence must always be bigger than your fear.

To be perfectly honest, we are all born with the potential for fear and a little fear is normal. The problem arises when you experience fear that overwhelms and paralyzes your very existence. I know first hand how fear can lock your growth in a shell of defeat but I was able to overcome my fear when bravery was my only option. When the instructor pilot exited the aircraft we knew if he could not simply take the controls and tell us what we did wrong. The reality of him no longer being in helicopter to save us made the fear scream louder than ever.

There was no one to blame for failure or credit for success which meant that I had to bring my A game. It is perfectly normal to rely on people and things as crutches instead of taking ownership for the outcome. This is the "fear factor crutch" which acts as a safety net just in case something goes wrong. To overcome this hurdle, you must learn to launch into the deep-head first.

"In order to bridge the gap from ambition to achieving your plans, you must deal with the causes of your personal fear factor."

In order to bridge the gap from ambition to achieving your plans, you must deal with the causes of your personal fear factor. When fear intercepts your plan, your ability to execute is jeopardized. When enthusiasm disappears passion fades and everything is at a stand still. This may lead to feelings of disappointment in yourself as you waste valuable time wondering what happened. I have visited the pit stop of fear several times on my path to success and, I can honestly say that unchecked fear is the thief of confidence. When you allow your confidence to be stolen its common to withdraw because of embarrassment. When self-esteem bottoms out most people isolate and remain in hibernation until the feelings of defeat disappear. Once an individal feels comfortable to emerge from a loss to fear they may walk around hoping that no one remembers to ask about your once again failed project. The only way to overcome fear is to identify the triggers and commit to your success.

Identifying & Overcoming Fear

This fearful behavior is reinforced each time something is avoided due to fear. That fear is then transferred to all areas of your life. The erosion of your self-confidence simultaneously affects your self-esteem. The self-critic dominates your thought process and self doubt inevitably moves in as one begins to experience what many term "fear of success". If the fear is not addressed it continues to sabotage your every move.

Would you believe some people are actually afraid of success? This might sound strange but I guarantee you that it is true. Many are afraid of the responsibility of success and this alone keeps them from achieving greatness. It is easy to develop fear of success when comparison becomes apart of the puzzle. If you compare yourself with others it is normal to feel inferior. This will cause you to believe that no matter how much success you achieve, it will never stack up. When you begin to rationalize that even though you achieve all your goals, you still won't be able to find happiness and true contentment in your life.

The first way to identify fear it to recognize negative comparisons. When you compare in a negative way you measure your skills and dreams through someone elses' abilities. Once you identify a comparison it is vital that you immediately release the thoughts. Any thought that you hold onto will eventually become apart of your mindset. I am sure great things in your life start by just taking this first step.

When you compare in a negative way you measure your skills and dreams through someone elses' abilities.

Without that first step, nothing is possible. But by taking that first step, the impossible suddenly becomes possible. That is the secret of achieving success. I like to call this the crawl, walk, and run phase of facing your fears. You must crawl and acknowledge that fear has a grip on your life. While you are metaphorically crawling, you begin to get upset about how fear has prevented you from accomplishing so much in life. You must become radically opposed to being fearful as it stiffens your growth. You are in the middle stage of overcoming fear. As you begin to move into the walking stage, your confidence levels are improving and now you are holding your head high. You are putting the past behind you and are not allowing any doubts to set in your mind. You are confident, strong and know you are a walking success. You are almost ready for the running stage of facing your fears. As you face your fear and realize everyone has to overcome some sort of challenge, you begin to look at fear differently. Now fear is a means to an end. You accept fear and it motivates you to move to your next level. You are not afraid of fear...you accept fear and press forward. In fact, you say to yourself...thank you fear for pushing me to my next level. You know you are in the running phase when you invite fear and it makes you a stronger person. This inevitably will cause you to go the extra mile which will set you up for the next level of success.

The flight instructor I mentioned previously was not at all fearful of leaving us to fly alone. Instead he was confident that he provided us with the tools to fly safely with confidence. This is the second way you can overcome your fear. It's important to stand in confidence when you have done everything within your power to be successful. It is impossible to experience fear and confidence at the exact same time. Imagine standing in the mirror feeling confident in your appearance. When you focus on confidence there is no fear of not measuring up. Remember to identify any triggers along the way that hinder your confidence and feed your fear.

Have you ever wondered why you let one, little emotion stand in the way of accomplishing so many things in your life? It is nearly impossible to achieve what you desire in life if you are unwilling to do what it takes. When you identify and overcome your fear you gain access to what others only dream about. You have to write your vision and know all things will work together as long as you just believe. Fear has a tendency to stomp on your current beliefs and try to dismember and disorganize your thought process. If you do not find the courage to overcome fear you give up your dreams of being successful.

Greg Provenzano gives you an interesting definition of fear. According to him, fear is the single biggest obstacle that stands in the way of where people are today and where they hope to be. Great definition by a multi-millionaire isn't it? Greg is the kind of person who never lets something small like fear stand in his way. He knows exactly how to overcome fear of failure and made a bold decision empower others. Greg has proven this idea through the courageous business decisions made throughout his life. People who are unafraid to fight for their dreams have benefitted greatly from his generosity. The possibility of becoming a successful Independent Business Owner is now a reality because of the fearless actions of one man.

When you choose to make your dreams of being financially independent come true, you learn how to overcome fear of the unknown. There are many lessons to be learned from jumping into the ocean with your big dreams. If you must fear something it should be trying something new instead of fear of the opinions of others. When you decide to touch the incredible feeling of

"Dare to be one of the extraordinary people who live on earth and have the guts to face fear daily."

flying high in the clouds of your big dreams, you definitely need to know how to overcome fear of failing. The process may not be easy but once you acknowledge your fears, it becomes the begining of a new chapter. Dare to be one of the extraordinary people who live on earth and have the guts to face fear daily. Throw out the negative thoughts and believe in yourself enough to overcome fear of failure. There is no loss in overcoming fear!

Navigate

What is your biggest fear?

What can you do today to overcome this fear?

Fear will prevent you from reaching your destination and must be overcome if you want to succeed in anything.

In order to grow, one must become uncomfortably brave even if it makes you sweat!

*Be sure to review the Questions to consider & Points to ponder to record your answers in the Rising through the rank's workbook

GO THE EXTRA MILE

An important principle of success in all walks and occupations of life is a willingness to " Go The Extra Mile ". This can be easily defined as the rendering of service far better than the amount for which one is paid. This also includes giving it with a positive mental attitude. Search wherever you will for a sound argument against this principle and you will not find it, nor will you find a single instance of enduring success without it. You will stand out like a sore thumb by doing something extra without any motives.

A few years ago, my wife and I were traveling to the Republic of Dominica. We had great room service and the butler who attended our care was very astute and hospitable. He went the extra mile in taking care of us. We were elated because he was not slack nor did he seemed burdensome by our requests and needs. He made sure we were taken care of in every aspect even when it was not his call of duty. We told him how thankful we were to have met him and how grateful we were to have him as a steward. He was so pleased at our kind words toward him. We visited the Republic of Dominica three years later and this same employee was now the manager of the resort. Going the extra mile, caused him to rise through the ranks and land him success.

Most people will not oppose doing nice things for others. When going the extra mile, you are setting yourself apart from others. People will begin to recognize what you are doing and if done on a consistent basis, they will realize this is your innate nature. Going the extra mile not only establishes your work ethic but it sends a message to others that you are person who preservers. The reality is that most people hate their jobs, are not happy with their supervisors and can't wait to leave the 9-5 work environment. One of the ways to set you apart is to realize you are there with a purpose. Take each day with a grain of salt and learn from your colleagues, supervisor and peers alike. Make sure you do not allow a grudge or bitterness to set in your heart when things do not go your way...just learn from the experience and go the extra mile. Your job is not your final destination! Maybe your job is a stepping stone or a milestone to your next promotion. Emulate perseverance.

I read about someone who recognized the value of going the extra mile later on in life. He always loved playing a guitar and he was in a few bands when he was younger and noted that it was a lot of work! Eventually, he decided that it wasn't worth working so hard so, he stopped playing. He changed his path enrolled into a university, and became an accountant! Fast forward twenty years, he realized that it's easy to give up and not work towards what you REALLY want, but it's not rewarding. He hated his job and his life. Eventually, he picked his guitar back up, recorded himself playing, put it up on YouTube, and now he is working every day (in the hours after his accounting job) to make the dream of playing guitar for a living come true. He is now willing to persevere and go the extra mile and work towards that dream and goal that he is passionate about.

"It's never too late to put in the work towards your desires and dreams.."

If you want more out of life, it doesn't matter what age you are or where you are in life, you can do what you need to do to have the success you want right now. It's never too late to put in the work towards your desires and dreams. In fact, sometimes it pays to wait because you have more life experience that helps you keep doing the work you need to do consistently.

Harry Potter fans know all-to-well who J.K. Rowling is. She created a hero from a concept that was rejected by several publishers, including the one who finally came around to publishing it. Before the success of her books, she went through a divorce which forced her to rely on state aid. Her experiences helped shape her stories, and she was relentless in her pursuit of getting published. Fans should be grateful that she persevered as the stories made her one of the most successful women in the entertainment industry. It's difficult not to be enchanted by her stories. The advantages of the habit of going the extra mile are definite and understandable.

The habit brings the individual to the favourable attention of those who can and will provide opportunities for self-advancement. You probably have read about successful people online or in magazines. A major trait they all share is one of perseverance.They kept going then and continue to keep going. You will hear others refer to them as machines or make references to the Energizer Bunny. Throughout history, we find great stories of perseverance. Many wonder why these people didn't simply give up. Often, it was because they believed in something far greater than themselves. They had an end goal constantly in mind; an unwavering manner of achieving their dream. It tends to make one indispensable, in many different relationships. It can also enable command for more than average compensation of personal services. If mental growth and physical skill improve perfection of the craft may occur; thereby adding to one's earning capacity. This protects one against the loss of employment when it is scarce and in a position to command high-quality jobs.

If mental growth and physical skill improve perfection of the craft may occur; thereby adding to one's earning capacity.

What does it mean to go the extra mile? To persevere? It means to work hard, and be consistent with your efforts. For instance, if you want to be a millionaire, you need to be willing to go the extra mile. It's not easy to become a millionaire. If it was, everyone would be doing it! You need to be willing to do the work. You need to be willing to invest in your education and learn what needs to be learned to earn money and then invest it to reach the kind of wealth that you want.Those who have not seen what it can do have a difficult time understanding the power of perseverance. Its power is something that has changed lives, changed countries, and sometimes even changed the world.

The power of preserverance

Preserverance brings hope to those who need it and power to those who pratice it. Whenever a batter strikes out at bat, it is perseverance that keeps him coming back to the plate and taking another swing. Every time he steps onto that plate he hopes for a home run. This hope is fueled by, and at the same time fuels his perseverance. One of the reasons why perseverance is so powerful is because of its direct connection to hope.

Preserverance brings hope to those who need it and power to those who pratice it.

It would be almost impossible to cover a subject on perseverance or successful people without mentioning Steve Jobs. He was the epitome of someone who would stop at nothing to succeed. Jobs started out as a nerdy kid in his garage. As a kid, he created a device that tricked the public phone system into giving people free phone calls. He sold these devices to many people for a profit. While not exactly legal, it was inventive. Luckily, his future endeavors went on the path of legitimacy.

Jobs started Apple computers with his school friend Steve Wozniak. The company was a success initially, but then the two had differences on how the company should be run. These disagreements eventually led to Jobs being let go.

Jobs later created a powerhouse with NeXT Computers and the struggling Apple company bought it to bring back Jobs into the management mix. Jobs was an extremely driven person all the way up to his death.

Perseverance is so powerful because it allows you to hang on to your desires. It helps you focus on what you want most until you finally achieve your prized victory. When you stick to something, constantly trying, and getting up each time you fall, you are bound to get it. You will receive that which you desire. When you reach that point where no person can tell you that it will not happen, then you know for certain that it will happen. This is the power of perseverance. It's the power of focus and the power of an undeniable promise that you will get what you want.

It is widely believed that Thomas Edison tried his lightbulb idea at least 10,000 times before getting it to work. Whether this is entirely true or the stuff of Urban Legends is anyone's guess. What is true is that he was someone who persevered. He would keep working at his projects until he made them work. He was also an early adopter of mass production which helped lower costs and allowed many to access his products. He founded General Electric, which continues to be one of the largest corporations in the world.

Preserverance preserves your youth and legacy. If you have the will to win, and the want for that which you desire, then nothing can stand in your way. Preserverance keeps you youthful and focused on the legacy you wish to leave behind. Perseverance has the power to make up for talent, genius, and age as it makes you courageous, and capable.

Without a persistent attitude, you are likely to fall at the first hurdle.

Whenever you set out on any road to success, perseverance is key to obtaining it. Without a persistent attitude, you are likely to fall at the first hurdle. Do you think anyone has it easy when they decide to venture out on a life of abundance and prosperity? If it was that simple, there would be no challenge and everyone would experience the virtue of all that it has to offer. We are tested every part of the way and that is just the way it is. Among the drive, determination and a consistent attitude, perseverance is key to being successful.

You cannot gain success overnight and that is why perseverance is key to being successful and you have to realise how important it is to attain it. Look at all the great achievers from the past and present. You will see an uncanny resemblance to all the attributions they possess in their pursuit of great success. There is no shortcut to success and while you can see get rich quick systems popping up all over the place, you are only fooling yourself to believe and depend on such pie in the sky fantasies. Unless you win on the lotto, find black gold on your land or unearth some lost treasure, you will have to rely on your own endeavour and toil, if you want to achieve real success.

The evidence is there for all to see, where real struggles and a strength of character were a part of extremely successful individuals that would never accept failure and giving up was never a part of their overall plan. Beethoven,Thomas Edison, Nelson Mandela, Michael Dell, Lance Armstrong are just a few names you might know who had their own struggles, but understood that perseverance is key to being successful and successful they all were, with a vision for what they all wanted to accomplish.

When initially applying for aviator school, I was not accepted into the program. I could not understand the reasoning because I met all the requirements and excelled in the Army Flight Aptitutde and Skills Examination (AFAST). This baffled me but it did not defeat me because I was determined to become an aviator. I continually dreamt about being a pilot and constantly read more books on aviation and aerodynamics. My desire to fly was fueled by the non acceptance into the program. Eventually, I met pilots who began to take me under their wings and insisted that I did not give up on my dreams although I was stacked against the odds. Without their knowledge they became my mentors. I am happy to say that I did not give up on my aspirations…I persevered and became an Apache Longbow Pilot in Command. If you didn't understand its power before, hopefully you do now. With hope, and focus, as a bulldozer for obstacles and a promise of achievement on its side; perseverance is actually one of the most powerful forces any person can have.

How can I go the extra mile?

It's never too late to put in the work towards your desires and dreams.

Preserverance brings hope to those who need it and power to those who pratice it.

.

*Be sure to review the Questions to consider & Points to ponder to record your answers in the Rising through the rank's workbook

⑦

DEVELOP YOUR GIFT

Caution, if you are not willing to develop your gifts, do not continue reading. Knowing how to develop your gifts is one of the secrets known by successful leaders all across the country. Why do you think some of them pay $50K for personal mentors! Developing your gifts not only increases your income but it enables you to better assist others. This allows the advantage of moving across the sea of chaos to a sea of prosperity. Rising through the ranks can't become any simpler than this!

Let's not get anything twisted, you must also add passion to the process of development of your gifts and talents. When you are passionate about a particular thing, you are able to lock into the ability to "flow" naturally. Well known speakers such as Tony Robins or Lisa Nicoles, have developed their gift so well that they are able to deliver an effective message without notes. They command the stage and although they may have reviewed the previously prepared notes behind the scenes, publicly they are as smooth as silk. They are able to engage others and convey their messages clearly because they are locked into their natural flow. This is an example of the level of discipline needed to allow your passion to shine through to new levels . You must be passionate about your gifts and it must become natural as breathing air. If you develop your gifts, your success will sky rocket! If your gifts (talents) are not developed you will go to your grave having lived a life of "I wish I could have". So many people are living day by day fulfilling the dreams of others while neglecting their own purpose in life. What you have inside of you needs to come to fruition…now. Make a commitment to take one step towards developing your gifts and I guarantee life will change. It is important to allow passion to be the reinforcement to prevent further delays.

Before I became a pilot I knew it was my passion and I had to be willing to develop it. I wanted to fly the Apache helicopter so desperately that I had dreams of flying. After doing the hard work and going through various process I was promoted to the rank of Staff Sergeant. That alone was not enough to qualify me for my dream so I had to continue the development process. My passion was high but the requirements were higher and I could not fly as an enlisted soldier. Being a sergeant wasn't enough so I continued my development process and became an officer. Sometimes along the development journey you may see that the requirements set a high bar. When this happens it is a personal responsibility to fully commit to the development journey. When you commit to your development you show the world that you are serious about your gift and ready to do whatever it takes to grow.

I took charge of my success by learning the military environment rank structure and jargon. I even joined the honor (color) guard to set myself apart. This gave me exposure to high ranking individuals like Lieutenant General (LTG) Kenneth Wykle. I even sung at his retirement ceremony which set me apart from others. Nothing was beneath me because I knew that it was all a part of my plan to develop my gifts! I relocated to Ft. Rucker, AL for flight training while maneuvering through the ranks. While in Ft Rucker I studied, took examination and passed with flying colors, but it didn't stop there! Before long, I was in the office of LTG Kenneth Wyke and he endorsed me to become a pilot of the prestigious Apache Longbow helicopter. He asked me what did I want to do in the future. I unequivocally told him that I wanted to be a pilot. After he heard my response, he wrote a letter of recommendation that would change the course of my life. Needless to say, I passed flight school, became a pilot

"...small things can become big dreams if you are passionate about them..."

in command and flew over 1,800 combat hours in Iraq. The development journey does not compare to the gratitude I experience for my passion and gifts! Remember, small things can become big dreams if you are passionate about them.

Helping others to grow and pursue their passion is a sure way to develop your gift. Learning to help others get to their next level, broadcasts your learning curb on another dimension. Believe it or not, helping others actually helps you. This is paramount to your success and talents. This simple step is in line with the well known a law of sowing and reaping. It is an universal law that most successful people use at their discretion. In fact, if this law becomes habitual, your success rate is exponentially increased.

The importance of developing your gifts are two fold. First, it allows room for self-improvements. In order to develop what is already inside of you, you must become acutely aware of your abilities and ways to improve who you are. Secondly, developing your gifts, gives you an opportunity to fine tune your talents. There may be fears you must overcome and the only way to move ahead is to conquer that thing called fear. This is vital to developing your gifts and talents.

Let's revisit some of the most influential and successful people across the country. Oprah Winfrey believes what she gives to others will come back to her 100 fold and probably donates and gives more to charity than anyone I know. She is living in the universal law of sowing and reaping. Her apparent success not a coincidence and the secret is in plain view. The development of her rise to wealth was derived from her desire and execution of helping others grow. Think of Bill and Melinda Gates, they are well known philantropist and leaders of the world. They wholeheartedly believe in helping others succeed. Their motto is "All Lives have Equal Value". This is why they are super successful. Both Oprah and the Gates have not only developed their gifts, but fine tuned it into perfection. It is now their "norm" to give and help others. I could list many others who are philantropist but I think you get the gist of what I am saying.

Passions & Gifts

Passion is your fuel, it motivates you to press on and propels you up the mountain of your dreams and goals. Have a passion for life, for people, for animals, for your causes and your convictions. Passion realized yields giftings unleashed. Once you realize your appetite for

"Your passion can lead you to a position of being a champion for those who have great needs"

development you will be nearly unstoppable. Your passion can lead you to a position of being a champion for those who have great needs and can't do anything about it themselves. I flew the planes with passion which assisted in my rise through. Make the personal choice to unveil your passion and speak with passion, teach with passion, lead with passion, love with passion, play with passion, and enjoy with passion. Someone who is passionate is intriguing to watch and to listen to. They are usually energizing to be around. They put great care into each and every detail of what they have passion for. A passionate musician plays a piece over and over until it is perfection for her and the audience. Each sound is perfectly crafted and resonates purely, hauntingly, and brilliantly. Every song on the album may not be perfect, and sometimes it misses the mark, but we recognize the passion and are moved by the story told, how it was done and perhaps why it was done. Passion draws people in, and to you. They want to be part of that passion. They want to be motivated as you are. They want to touch that passion, and embrace it. Passion lifts people up to a new level, which they can feel for themselves and from you. Passion encourages and fosters new energy into people and projects. Everyone wants to feel passion for something.

When you come to roadblocks in life, your passion helps you to overcome each and every halt. When there is passion involved, you have a need to move forward. The focus shifts to reaching beyond every expectation towards the fulfillment of dreams and goals. Pit stops can refresh your passion for life or an aspect of your work. It also places a responsibility on you to dig deep within yourself to find what really motivates and captivates you. Once you do the next step becomes finding brand new aspects of your passion or your love that you had not seen before. Once developed the passion and gifts can open new doors and opportunities to gravitate towards other passionate people. You become the leader of your life by creating new paths with your passion and deep desires.

A person who does not realize and develop passion can wallow in the low points of life. When gifts are not developed and passion is not fulfilled it can lead to difficulties finding the meaning in . This is because passion gives meaning and meaning yields purpose. You must discover the passions of your life to thrive personally and professionally. Uncovering passion requires patience and courage in addition to creativity. Most people never really uncover their passion because of the amount of patience it requires.

Before you can develop your gift you need to ask three questions to yourself and answer them truthfully in your journal:

Who Am I?
What Is My Passion?
What Am I Called To Do?

Once you have answered the questions start the passion process by doing things that you enjoy doing: cooking, painting, photography, performing, etc. When you find a certain aspect that you are really enjoying, spend more time doing it. Learn about it, develop your interest and your knack for it, and find ways to become more involved with your hobby or pastime. When you start to become passionate about something, then you want to spend as much of your time as you can by being in and around it. You develop desire to learn everything you can about it and, you want to be with other people who have your same interests or passions. Their passion and love fuels your passion.

Take care of the small details with the same care and regard as if it were a great big event and you will move up the mountain with a steady sure foot. Passionate leaders recognize passionate people, and the details of passion, and they hire and promote passionate workers, and create openings for those people. You can be passionate about anything and remember that anything becomes something to the right person. Small or large, if you are passionate about it, you can see huge results; your passion can take you to great places. You can make your living by doing what you love to do and if properly developed someone may want to pay you for what you love to do. If you can't find a boss that loves what you do, be your own boss. Don't be afraid to start your own company if you are passionate enough about what you are doing. Either way, your passion will open a new door. Other people will become aware of your passion and your services. There are many customers out there looking for your services; you just have to find, target, and market to them. It is not always easy to start from scratch, and it can be particularly difficult when you are creating a new niche. But, if you can sustain yourself during the grow and development process your client base will expand while enabling you to create your desired flow.

"If you develop your gift you can rise through a rank that you create and control!"

When you cannot rise through the ranks created by others explore your passion to create your own! This can only happen when your skills are appropriately developed to assist in leading the life that you desire for yourself. Many times you cannot do it on your own, and that is when your passion will lead you to a partner or a team that has your same passion and can help. When you find your team it is vital to develop your leadership skills. The team can become stronger as you work together because your passion is the driving force. Even if your goals change a little the same underlying passion should remain and can keep the wheels turning. What you thought was impossible on your own has now become a possibility and you are rewarded for it. Your life, and their lives, begin to be satisfying all because you took charge and developed your gifts.

It is thrilling when you begin to watch your dreams become realities and, share your victory with the team you create. When you do this the team will develop a reputation of excellence and passion. You will see that more creative and energetic people are drawn to the team because they like what they are seeing. Because of that, your team will be able to do more than they could before, and complete additional projects. Your team will be able to scale impossible heights in a very short period of time, and you will reach the greatest pinnacles of success that you have ever dreamed about. If you develop your gift you can rise through a rank that you create and control!

Navigate

Take a moment to reflect your personal passion and gift(s) to identify ways you can create or navigate through your rise.

What is your big or small thing(gift)?

What is your big dream?

What are you the most passionate about?

Passion is your fuel, it motivates you to press on and propels you up the mountain of your dreams and goals.

If you develop your gift you can rise through a rank that you create and control!

*Be sure to review the Questions to consider & Points to ponder to record your answers in the Rising through the rank's workbook.

⑧

BELIEVE IN YOURSELF.

Let's revisit the baker I mentioned in the introduction. Imagine visiting the store they own, you walk in and inhale the aroma. Your senses are excited to experience the bread but you can't quite figure out what to select. The various breads line the insides of the display case and everything appears delicious. As fate would have it the baker walks out from the kitchen and greets you. Immediately you notice that the baker does not make eye contact and lacks confidence in the products. The baker is dressed in the appropriate attire and the atmosephere is set but there is no belief in the quality of the product. Your mind begans to shift and you no longer want to experience the bread. The scent that invited you in now becomes the aroma that pushes you away. Eventually you decide to purchase an item anyway but your confidence in the store and the quality of the product never returns. Now imagine if the baker would have been confident.

What if the baker would have explained the time and dedication that went into each delectable loaf of bread? I am sure that instead of just one item you may have purchased more. If confidence was present you would have enjoyed the item and told others of the delightful bakery. When you believe in yourself you literally send a message to everyone you encounter. The message conveys confidence and control while opening the door for your attainable rise.

If you don't believe in yourself then who will? If you want to become a magnet for your rise you must saturate every action with self belief. When you believe in yourself, confidence exudes from your pores. It is your responsibility to believe the things you say for them to manifest in your life. A person who believes in what he or she is saying is someone people are willing to follow. When I received the initial denial for flight school I had to make a personal choice to believe in myself beyond the no. This is a challenge for most people because no is often seen as rejection. Self belief interprets no as the invitation to try again a different way. I dug deeper and partnered with a mentor who could co- sign my self belief with their seal of approval. This was a vital step to my rise because it placed a responsibility on me to not only believe in myself but to also value my skills. I knew what I had to offer because I put in the work and my cosigner could see the improvements. Link with those who add to your self belief in a healthy way, and avoid those who criticize you for daring to be confident. Lacking self-confidence can affect your life drastically as it means you may miss out on opportunities that are presented to you.

Wealth & Confidence

Have you ever wondered why wealthy people always seem so confident and self assured. I have observed that wealth and confidence are synonymous and normally, you don't find one without the other. Self-confidence is a pre-requisite for financial success. It gives you the courage to say things you would not normally say. When you are confident you have no problem asking for a raise or quoting a client a fee that might raise their eyebrows. Confidence allows you to say no to someone, even if that no might make someone unhappy or even angry with you. Confidence allows you to say yes to someone, when you are confident you can deliver on a promise.

You may have encountered the quote "success breeds success" or "success breeds confidence" but how about confidence breeding success? If you act confidently (regardless of whether you actually feel confident or not) you will find that people will start respecting you and listening to you, thus giving you the momentum to be confident in your own right. Even if you haven't encountered great success yet, there is no reason you can't bluff a little and act like you have. Confidence is a magnet in the best sense of the word."

"Even if you haven't encountered great success yet, there is no reason you can't bluff a little and act like you have!"

So, Why are financially successful people able to present an image of self confidence? As simple as it sounds, confidence changes your behavior and the behavior of those you deal with. More importantly, people love dealing with confident people. They flock to them like a moth to a flame. Insecure people seek after confident people and will follow them, bend to their will, alter their schedules to accommodate them, do favors for them, try to befriend them and generally give them whatever they want. On the other hand, confident people usually get what they want. They can move mountains to achieve their objectives and goals, with their tribe of followers doing the heavy lifting. Honestly, transition is easier and your goals for rising become attainable when you are confident. It also breeds financial success and good leaders always exude a confidence that creates followers.

Everyone, even the wealthiest individuals, experience adversity in their every day lives. Adversity can indeed create stress but a healthy dose of confidence can help you deal with adversity. I once read about a wealthy person who said when faced with adversity or stress he says to himself over and over: "Water off a Duck's Back". When someone pressed him as to what this actually meant he explained how the feathers of a duck are water proof and the water just rolls easily off the feathers. He sees adversity and stress as nothing more than water and visualizes it rolling easily off his back. What he really means is that he does not let stress get the best of him. Because he is so confident, he believes he can overcome any adversity or set-back.

Being an assured and confident person has many benefits, in personal lives as well as in employment, career development and business. Whatever your aims and ambitions in life may be, building your self confidence will play an important role in achieving success and overcoming any fears or crisis of confidence you may have along the way.

Positive attitude creates the fertile ground for confidence to grow and flourish. Most people with negative thoughts decrease their possibility of success almost immediately. This is because positive thinking can provide a regular boost to progress. Negativity robs you of the ability to think yourself through difficult periods during the navigation process. The easiest way to accelerate your achievements is to think highly of yourself and your gifts. It is important to remember that self confidence can sometimes be misplaced. Egocentric people often provide examples of this. They tend to display a high level of confidence which, if examined, is a mix of arrogance and self deceit. This particuliar mix of personality traits, while masquerading as self confidence, will not necessarily lead to success.

It can also be true that somebody who is not naturally self confident, can suddenly achieve what is perceived as a big success. Instead of revelling in the glory of their achievement, shyness and a crisis of confidence can affect this type of person. This may force them to hide from the basking glory of their success. The unconfident baker provides a prime example of this.

Whether you are naturally self assured or not, it is important that you develop a harmonious relationship between your confidence levels and the route to success you are taking. If they are not synchronized and in harmony, then overconfidence may eventually unhinge your progress, or lack of confidence may lead to a fall just as you have reached the top of the ladder. Confidence requires the conscious investment in self for appropriate development and display.

Be you & Build You

Hopefully you can agree with me in saying that we tend to invest in many things that do not give a great return on investment (ROI). Investing in yourself is one of the best ROI you can have. Whether it's investing in learning a new skill, developing yourself personally or professionally, or even hiring a coach, you need to give to yourself **first** before you can give to others. It is your responsibility to take the time to develop your gifts and talents, so

"... investing in yourself is an example of how you plan to seek improvements in your life.."

you can best serve others. Why is investing in yourself so powerful? Simply stated, investing in yourself is an example of how you plan to seek improvements in your life.

When you Invest in yourself emotionally, physically, spiritually and financially, you to enable the best version of yourself to thrive. When you are the best version of yourself, you will be an attraction magnet to others! Investing in yourself, sends a powerful message to yourself and others around you. You are essentially saying, the value and potential that I possess, is important enough to me that I'm going to give it the energy, space and time to grow. You place value on what you believe is beneficial to your growth and development.

When you're willing to say yes, and take that leap of faith and invest in yourself, things will start to happen. Invest in being the best you by building up your best parts. This will have an undeniable and evident impact on your rise. Take a moment to review the five incredible ways that you can invest in yourself. Keep an open mind and try to outline one or two that stand out to you.

5 Ways to Invest in yourself

1. Attend local workshops to expand your knowledge. You might start at the local library and ask for the next business opportunity workshop. By attending these local events, you open yourself to more opportunities and allow yourself to meet and interact with like-minded persons. Find your local chamber of commerce and join their business page, this will provide you with other contacts as well.

2. Pratice healthy nutritional habits. Most of us know the importance of eating healthy, but many do not heed what they already know. Taking care of your health is vital to your success. If you want to become a public speaker, your image means a lot. You want to look your best and feel your best. Eating the right

foods will cause you to have burst of energy before walking on stage.

3. Exercise regularly. Most people avoid working out because they don't have "time" in their schedule. If you manage your time effectively, a great work out will enhance your confidence and give you that extra energy when others are wore out. Studies have shown that people who exercise on a regular basis are more likely to feel happier. This will cause you to become excited about your new opportunity every morning.

4. Stay positive. You have the ability to choose to be happy. Do you look at the glass half empty or half full? Even if something does not go your way, try to focus on the positive. Remember there could be worst things happening in your life, but if you believe you are on the right track, great things will follow after you.

5. Find a mentor/coach. We have discussed repeatedly the importance of finding a mentor and this could not be reiterated enough. Look for someone who is successful in your field of study and humbly ask to become their mentee. This mentor will be able to assist you in putting all of your strategies into action.

A coach is your partner in success. It is their job to assist you in creating and implementing your success plan, so you can become the best that you can be.

When you invest in yourself, a world of opportunities will open up for you. And, if you have a business where you sell your services, you must know that no one will invest in you until you invest in yourself first.

Seal the deal

Now let's be honest, have you ever bought something that you did not particularly need and after the fact you said to yourself, "why did I just buy that?" It's sometimes called buyer's remorse. More likely than not, you purchased the new item because you were "sold" on the person and not the item. This why it is imperative that you believe in yourself. You are selling who you are, you are selling your words, you are selling your character and more importantly you are selling yourself. Once people believe in you and know your motives are pure, you will not have any problems selling to others. It's called trust. Believing in yourself make others want to trust you. You are now branding who you are! This means everything you do and say must be a credible resource.

People don't buy things because they need them, many times people purchase items because they liked the sales person. Why are some sales representatives better at sales than others? Some salesmen can sell swamp land on a farm and make a profit by doing so. It's because they believe in themselves and understand the art of selling. Examples of profitable people who have incredible self confidence are the timeshare representatives. You may know someone who have purchased a timeshare unexpectedly. In fact, these salesmen are very good at selling and if by chance you don't purchase from them you end up leaving feeling guilty. The family had no intentions of buying a timeshare but after speaking to a convincing and persuading salesman, the family was signing a contract for a vacation home. The representative pursued the emotions of the family member and made them realize how important travel and or vacations were to them. You must have the same tenacity as the sales rep when it comes to your next promotion. Believe great things are awaiting you because you not only deserve it but you expect it to happen.

If you look at successful people, you will usually find they have great self confidence. That self assurance may have come as a result of their success, but often, a degree of confidence in one's own ability is present before the road to success even commences. Once out on that open road, then success and self confidence may ride in tandem, each providing the fuel for the other's journey.

So how do you get back on the road to success? First, you should start focusing on the positive things you have already achieved and make it a weekly task, or even daily if necessary, to get you back on track. Pay attention to your strengths and your weaknesses in order to be prepared for all situations. Second, once you start working towards your large goal, then you can break it down into smaller, more attainable goals. By doing this you will be able to celebrate your achievements along the way - regardless of their size - thereby boosting your self-confidence enabling you to move ahead.

Inching out of your comfort zone is the only way of achieving sure-fire success. Take a deep breath and just go for it! Your confidence, once developed, will definitely lead you where you want to go. You must understand the importance of building your confidence. While building your confidence it is vital to invest in what can help you improve your confidence. Finding mentors, reading on the

"...Inching out of your comfort zone is the only way of achieving sure-fire success."

subject in which you want to become the expert are examples.

Generally speaking, confidence and success exist in environments of progressive harmony. If you can work on steadily improving your confidence, you can do so owing that over the years that growing assurance and self belief will be a strong support on each step up the ladder of success.

Even somebody with a low self esteem or suffers from shyness has the potential to reach their level of success that they dream of. Keep your ambitions and inhibitions in perspective, then succeeding in the long term is very much within the bounds of possibility.

Some people try to lose weight by saying, "My new year resolution is to lose X amount of weight." They already know within their heart it's just talk. They feel good saying what they want to accomplish, but never commit to executing what it takes to lose the weight. Year after year these resolutions are vainly made knowing it is just talk. I encourage you to stop wasting time and effort on things you are not going to accomplish. It is time to become accountable for what is spoken from your mouth and not waste any more valuable time with vain repetitions. When you change your perspective and believe everything that is spoken, improvements in your life can be made immediately.

Whether you are naturally self assured or not, it is important that you develop a harmonious relationship between your confidence levels and the route to success you are taking. If they are not synchronized and in harmony, then overconfidence may eventually unhinge your progress, or lack of confidence may lead to a fall just as you have reached the top of the ladder. Give yourself a chance to succeed.

Navigate

How can I believe in myself more?

Self belief interprets no as the invitation to try again a different way.

When you Invest in yourself emotionally, physically, spiritually and financially, you to enable the best version of yourself to thrive.

When you believe in yourself you literally send a message to everyone you encounter.

Epilogue:
THE CALL TO RISE

Take a moment to think of the success you wish to achieve. Now wrap your mind around the reality that it is possible! Again I remind you that everything starts with the mindset. If your mind has not been transformed then success will be harder to obtain. A new pathway must be created in your mental psyche to maintain the growth mindset. Once you do this visualization becomes easier because you are creating the environment for positive growth. When you began to mentally see your growth before it becomes a reality nothing will shake your belief in it. Cling to the visions when times are tough and growth seems challenging. As you are holding tight to the mental images of your rise remember to operate in integrity. This means doing the right thing… at all times.

Live your life as if someone is always watching and depending on you to restore the faith in humanity. When you wake up each day call forth the best you and do not yield to temptation. The more you hold yourself to a high moral standard the easier it will become to operate in it daily. This is important because there will be many test along the path to your rise. My personal test have led me to a deeper understanding of the power I possess to pursue my passions, enthusiastically. When you fully commit to you the test along the way may become opportunities to build integrity and maintain a growth mindset.

When I joined the military I was not fully aware of the challenges that would come with my decision to serve. I wish I could say I always did the right thing but we both know that would be a stretch. While I cannot say I was perfect I can say that I valued my integrity and the mentors that helped me develop it. If I would have leaned only on my limited mindset, visualizations and integrity I may have never reached my big goals. The easiest way to foster growth is by linking up with individuals who can pour into your life. Effective mentors are like the wind beneath the wings of a mentee. They will push you in unimaginable ways to reach new levels while facing your fears. They understand that insecurity is the only thing that can grow from fear. If I would not have linked with the right mentor I would not have received the letter of recommendation that changed my life. My goals began to become real when I took the steps outside of my fear to really connect. Not only did I connect with others but I took time to reconnect with myself to decide what I really wanted. I believe that we are all born with a measure of instinct, integrity and wisdom but is must be nurtured for growth.

Once I knew I wanted to rise, no matter what, I eliminated the fears that kept me still. There is no place for fear on the road to rising and once realized it must always be checked and deleted. One fearful thought could have caused me to crash the plane on my first interdependent adventure. Fear will always magnify the possibility of danger over the possibility of success but, do not feed your fear! Starve the thoughts that say you are not enough and nurture the visions that keep you going. This will require that you to go the extra mile. For me going the extra mile was doing more than just enough. I prepared for my success by developing my gift.

If you have a gift and do not develop it you rob yourself of an opportunity to grow. Keep in mind that it is impossible to be the best without evolving from novice to expert in your field. One cannot stay on level one forever and expect to be taken seriously. When I set my heart on becoming an apache pilot I started to educate myself because I knew that my time would come. When the day came I was prepared because I developed my passion and spent time nurturing my dreams. Every action was fueled by self-belief and reinforced in confidence. The confidence I held allowed me to move from one profession to another with boldness and excellence. The belief I had in my abilities was bigger than any doubt or obstacle.

When you believe in yourself it sends a message of confidence to the world. Self-belief can take you beyond your attainable visions to a world of endless possibilities. As cliché as it may sound there really is nothing impossible for those who believe. Be sure to carry the golden key of confidence daily as you navigate your next promotion. Trust me, you can actually achieve the success you dream of and live a life you enjoy.

I leave you with the wisdom of lessons learned on my journey and challenge you to continue on your own. As you navigate be sure to think yourself into your next level and began to see it in your mind. Walk in honor while heeding the wisdom of your guides. Face each fear and go the extra mile to develop your gift and increase your self-belief. Your rise is in your hands and I guarantee that life will change once you truly believe it. Rise dear reader, rise!

ABOUT THE AUTHOR

Anthony is a motivational speaker, author, pilot in command, and registered nurse, He offers a vast amount of expertise and knowledge to his audience. He joined the military at the young age of 17 to pursue his dreams of becoming a pilot. After 23 years of service, he retired from the U.S. Army at the age of 40. He holds a total of three degrees: two bachelors degrees, and one Master of Science Nursing (MSN) from Jacksonville University. His tours of duty include: Fort Jackson, South Carolina; Fort Rucker, Alabama; Fort Campbell, Kentucky; Fort Stewart, Georgia; Hunter Army Airfield, Savannah, Georgia; Fort Bragg, North Carolina; Fort Hood, Texas; Camp Humphreys, South Korea; and Baumholder, Germany. Additionally, he served two tours in Iraq; Operation Desert Shield/Desert Storm 1990- 1991, and Operation Iraqi Freedom III 2005-2006.

Awards:

Awards for meritorious accomplishments include:

Two Air Medals, Combat Aviation Badge, Senior Aviation Badge, Defense Service Medal, Air Assault Badge, Meritorious Service Medal, Joint Service Commendation Medal, Southwest Asia Service Medal w/ Bronze Service Star, Global War on Terrorism Service Medal, Kuwait Liberation Medal, and Joint Service Commendation Medals